philippians

A **SIMPLY BIBLE** STUDY

CARMEN BEASLEY

Copyright © 2018 | by Carmen Beasley

All rights reserved. No part of this publication may be reproduced, distributed, or transmitted in any form or by any means, including photocopying, recording, or other electronic or mechanical methods, without the prior written permission of the publisher, except in the case of brief quotations embodied in critical reviews and certain other noncommercial uses permitted by copyright law.

Scripture quotations are from the ESV® Bible (The Holy Bible, English Standard Version®), copyright © 2001 by Crossway, a publishing ministry of Good News Publishers. Used by permission. All rights reserved.

Journal and layout design by Melissa Trew.

To Jesus.

...who, though he was in the form of God, did not count equality with God a thing to be grasped, but emptied himself, by taking the form of a servant, being born in the likeness of men. And being found in human form, he humbled himself by becoming obedient to the point of death, even death on a cross. Therefore God has highly exalted him and bestowed on him the name that is above every name, so that at the name of Jesus every knee should bow, in heaven and on earth and under the earth, and every tongue confess that Jesus Christ is Lord, to the glory of God the Father.

PHILIPPIANS 2:5-11

And to women seeking after Him.

Have this mind among yourselves, which is yours in Christ Jesus...

PHILIPPIANS 2:5

I AM GLAD AND REJOICE
WITH YOU ALL. LIKEWISE
YOU ALSO SHOULD BE GLAD
AND REJOICE WITH ME.

PHILIPPIANS 2:17-18

table of *contents*

PHILIPPIANS | A **SIMPLY BIBLE** STUDY

INTRODUCTION

I.	**Welcome**	Sharing God's Story of **SIMPLY BIBLE**	1
II.	**Getting Started**	A Quick-Start Guide	7
III.	**Step by Step**	Unpacking the Inductive Method	13
IV.	**Lesson Samples**	Practice Lessons & Examples	21
V.	**In Context**	Examining the Context of Philippians	29
VI.	**Live Joyfully**	Becoming a *Doer* of the Word	35

STUDY CONTENT

I.	**Philippians 1**	41
II.	**Philippians 2**	57
III.	**Philippians 3**	73
IV.	**Philippians 4**	89
V.	**Final Thoughts**	Wrapping Up	105

APPENDIX

I.	**Leader Guide**	Maximizing the Small Group Experience	111

AND IT IS MY PRAYER THAT YOUR LOVE MAY ABOUND MORE AND MORE, WITH KNOWLEDGE AND ALL DISCERNMENT...

PHILIPPIANS 1:9

welcome!

SHARING GOD'S STORY OF **SIMPLY BIBLE**

AS A LITTLE GIRL, I ADORED COLORING BOOKS. Smooth, crisp, white pages displayed bold black lines of perfectly-drawn figures and characters. The spaces patiently awaited color. Fondly, I remember the joy of opening a new pack of crayons. The neat little rows of pointed tips colorfully peeked out and tantalized me as if to say, "Try to choose just one!" Creativity awaited. Or so I thought.

When my four children were small, through a friend of a friend, I was encouraged to forgo coloring books. My initial reaction was one of horror. "What? Coloring books are fun! That would be forgoing fun! Plain paper? How boring!" Okay, granted… my reaction was a little melodramatic, but I do remember thinking these thoughts.

Instead, this friend insisted that providing children with blank sheets of paper was the way to spur creativity. I could see the wisdom. Not to mention, a ream of paper was way cheaper than four new coloring books… and so, I gave it a try. For the most part, my children simply grew up with lots of plain white paper and a variety of colorful pencils, crayons, and markers.

SIMPLE TOOLS LED TO ARTISTRY. My kids learned to draw. Not just little stick figures in the middle of the page, but they learned to tell a story using a piece of paper. Masterpieces. (At least in my eyes!)

Now I'm sure no one ever saved one of my coloring book pages. Oh, for sure! Sometimes one landed on Grandma's refrigerator. However, right now, down in my basement, binders of pictures remain—pictures that my budding artists created more than twenty years ago. Why? These pictures were windows into their little hearts and minds. These illustrations tell stories. And this mom treasures them in her heart.

THIS IS THE GIST OF SIMPLY BIBLE. My heart desires to provide women with a "blank page" for reading and engaging with God and His Word. Rather than fill-in-the-blank questions, this study offers space to observe, understand, and apply. Don't get me wrong: just like coloring books, traditional Bible studies have their place. I wouldn't be the Bible student that I am today without them. And yet, I am rather fond of this series. Basic tools and gentle direction allow for a quiet place where women are able to engage their hearts, souls, and minds with the intention of listening to and knowing God. It's a place for women to relate and retreat with Him by sharing in His story—simply the Bible.

TO BE HONEST, **SIMPLY BIBLE** ALMOST DIDN'T HAPPEN. Yep! I've shared this story before, but here it goes again. It's sort of embarrassing.

After much prayer as a newly-appointed women's ministry director of my church, I was assessing the state of our women's ministries when God pointed me toward inductive Bible study. Inductive study implies investigating the Bible directly. That's it. And so, in my mind, the conversation looked like this:

Me: "Lord, You mean no video teaching and no fill-in-the-blank workbooks?"

God: "Yes. Take women directly to my Word."

Me: "Lord, women like to have a book in their hands, and preferably one from a well-known author."

God: "Use my Book."

So then, I obeyed. Ugh! I wish had immediately obeyed. Instead, and this is the embarrassing part, I played Gideon. I set my fleece out for God to prove His point, and I did it more than once. (If at this point you're doubting the validity of an author and a women's ministry leader who plays Gideon, I understand. You are welcome to return this book, no questions asked!) Instead of obeying, I purchased and reviewed every single Bible study available, at that time, on the gospel of John. Almost desperately, I was searching for something—anything—that would quietly and inductively walk women through that Gospel. One by one, God said "no." (Okay, it's not like God audibly spoke to me. But His Spirit has a way of getting His message across. You know what I mean?)

I continued to cry out to Him for a tool. Frankly, for years, as an experienced leader and Bible teacher, I had searched for a simple tool that does not require in-depth or extra training in order to teach or study inductively. I could not find one.

One day, while wrestling and praying over all of this, I sat down at my computer, opened a blank document, and began experimenting with the process of inductive study. I left my computer and went down to fix dinner. When I returned, I looked at what was on the paper and thought, "This works." Praise God! In perfect timing, He granted peace and direction.

He also led the way to Melissa Trew, a talented designer with a huge heart for God and His Word. She's a gift. Deftly, she takes this material, uses her God-giftedness, and turns it into something beautiful. Coffee-table worthy. Her designs are beyond anything I could begin to think or imagine. I'm grateful.

FINALLY, WHY INDUCTIVE STUDY? There are three main reasons, based on what today's woman says about Bible study:

FIRST: *"I feel inept. I know I should read the Bible. I want to, but I don't understand it."* Many women feel the same. With an influx of Bible study resources, we have relied on videos and books that give us the author's answers. It's easy to think we need an "expert" to intercede and interpret God's Word on our behalf. No doubt, there is a place for these resources, but we aren't to be dependent on them. We depend on God alone.

An old Chinese Proverb aptly says:

> Give a man a fish and you feed him for a day.
> Teach a man to fish and you feed him for a lifetime.

SIMPLY BIBLE is designed to equip women to "fish." By following the step-by-step framework, you can confidently approach God's Word. The inductive process of this journal eliminates my voice as much as possible, with the hopes that you can listen to God's voice alone. That's the beauty of inductive study: rather than listening to *an* author, we listen directly to *the* Author. My prayer is that, through His Word, we will experience the incredible joy and adventure of personal encounters with Him. And then? We share Him with others.

SECOND: *"I'm busy. Overwhelmed by demands. Life is crazy!"*
I know. I feel it too. This study should maximize time. Rather than spending time reading other books, watching videos, filling in the blanks, and checking Bible study off our "to-do" list, we skip the "middle-man" and go directly to God and His Word. Immediately, we relate with Him one-on-one.

Truly, this study can be catered to the needs of the busy woman who can barely scrape together ten minutes a day for Bible study. Yet, it can also fit the need of the woman who longs to linger and dig deeper into the Word. Kind of like scuba diving, you'll choose how deep you want to go and how far you'd like to roam.

THIRD: *"I need relationship. Do others care about me?"*
Today's younger woman is seeking connection. Her desire? To be seen, known, and loved. Video teaching often does not meet her expressed need because it takes time away from deeper relationship-building—both with Christ and with others. Although she is hungry to know, the bottom line is that she prefers personal interaction. And the discussion had better be relevant and meaningful, with no pat answers.

Concurringly, a generation of women my age is now dependent on video teachers and fill-in-the-blank studies, rather than dependent on God and His Word. Because of her dependency on these tools, a veteran Bible student is often ill-equipped to read the Bible for herself and even more ill-equipped to share her faith and God's Word with others.

Inductive study maximizes time and develops skills to focus on real relationship and interaction with God and others. Why **SIMPLY BIBLE**? To focus on the "relationship need" now felt acutely within women's ministries across the country.

CONSIDER FAST FOOD VERSUS A HOME-COOKED MEAL. Picking up fast food can be a treat. It's quick and easy. It's downright helpful to have someone else prepare and hand you the meal. Much of our Bible study resources are similar to "fast food." Someone else does the preparation and serves up a quick and easy word of encouragement. It's helpful, but it's not "home-cooked." Rarely would we serve fast food to friends or carry it to a potluck. The same holds true for feasting on God's Word. Inductive study allows for that special and intimate meal meant to be shared with others.

SO THAT'S A GOD-AT-WORK STORY. That's how **SIMPLY BIBLE** was birthed.

Since its inception, I've had the joy and privilege of watching women journal and seek God through these study workbooks. These journals are windows into hearts, souls, and minds growing with God. These notebooks tell stories. And although they are much too private for me to observe closely, I treasure them in my heart. If I could, I'd pile them up in my basement.

For each woman who has braved a **SIMPLY BIBLE** study, I am truly grateful. In a sense, there is a basement in my heart where memories of studying with you are tucked away. Thank you. You spur me on to dig deep into God's Word, to know and love Him and others more deeply.

If you are new, you've probably gathered by now that this study is different. And different often falls outside our comfort zones. The purpose of this journal is that you may confidently read, understand, and apply God's Word like you've never before experienced, using *simply* the Bible. It will require a commitment.

COMMIT. There's no "Oh, I'll just give it a try." Commit to see this study through to the finish.

If the inductive Bible study process is new to you, don't be intimidated. My first home-cooked meal didn't look or taste anything like my mom's meal. Cooking takes practice. Even after forty some years of cooking, most of what I cook tastes different from my mom's cooking. The same will be true for Bible study. Inductive study will take practice. Your study will look different from most others. You are unique and special. And so, your study insights and application will be unique. But, by the end, you will better know Jesus Christ, His Word, and your identity in Him. You are loved, valued, and treasured by an amazing God.

SO WELCOME TO **SIMPLY BIBLE**! And welcome to this particular series of Galatians, Ephesians, Philippians, and Colossians.

These epistles (or letters), written by the Apostle Paul, share a window into a heart set free to fully know and seek God. As we engage and share in God's Word, like Paul, may we yield our hearts and minds to God's heart, having the mind of Christ Jesus. And may He permeate and etch His fruit of love, joy, peace, patience, kindness, goodness, faithfulness, gentleness, and self-control onto the pages of our own hearts, for His glory.

I'm praying for you and with you.

With much love and joy,

getting *started*

A QUICK-START GUIDE TO **SIMPLY BIBLE**

getting *started*

AN INTRODUCTION TO INDUCTIVE BIBLE STUDY

Recently, a friend described **SIMPLY BIBLE** as "leaving behind her paint-by-numbers set for a blank canvas." Of course, her word picture melted my heart! But honestly, whether painting or digging into God's Word, using a blank canvas can be a little intimidating. It takes practice! Just as an artist learns a particular method and handles special tools to create a masterpiece, so do Bible study students.

The inductive Bible study method involves three basic steps that often overlap:
    (1) Observe
    (2) Interpret
    (3) Apply

Using the **SIMPLY BIBLE** format will help to paint a more thorough understanding of God's Word.

On the following pages, you will find a quick-start guide to **SIMPLY BIBLE**. This guide is followed by a more thorough explanation of the format and basic study tools. Take time to get a feel for them.

And then... dig in!

a quick start to *simply bible*

A STEP-BY-STEP GUIDE

READ	OBSERVE	INTERPRET
Read the passage. Try some of the following ideas to help you read carefully. (Highlighters and colored pencils are fun here!) • Read the passage in a different version. • Read it out loud. • Underline, circle, box, or highlight repeated words, unfamiliar words, or anything that catches your attention. • Listen to the passage while running errands. • Doodle or write out a verse in a journaling Bible.	As you read, write down your observations in this column. Simply notice what the Scripture *says*. This is your place for notes. Ideas include: • Ask questions of the text, like "who, what, when, where, or how." • Jot down key items: people, places, things. Mark places on a map. • Ask, "What does this Scripture passage say about Jesus?" • Note what took place before and after this passage. • Ponder. • Ask God if there is anything else He'd like you to notice.	In this column, record what the passage *means*. One way to interpret is to answer any questions asked during observation. Try to first answer these *without* the aid of other helps. Allow Scripture to explain Scripture. It often does. If the answers are not intuitive or easily found near the passage, other tools are available. Use boxes A, B, and C to identify a key word, define it, and look up a cross reference. This extra research will shed light on the meaning. IMPORTANT: Seek to understand what the passage meant to the author and his original readers. Try to look at the world through the eyes of early Christians.

PLEASE NOTE: The following boxes (labeled A, B, and C) are interpretation tools. These are meant to be used in unison with the "Interpret" column on the previous page to aid in interpreting Scripture. Most women find it helpful to complete these *before* interpreting. Find what's most helpful for you.

A KEY WORDS	**B** DEFINITIONS	**C** CROSS REFERENCES
When you notice a word that is repeated multiple times, is unfamiliar, or is interesting to you in any other way, record it here.	Here, record definitions of your key words. You can find the appropriate definitions by using: • a Bible concordance (defines words according to the original language) • a Bible dictionary • another translation	Note cross references. This is a solid way to allow Scripture to interpret Scripture. If your Bible does not include cross references, they can be found easily using web-based Bible resources.

Bible study tools like those listed above can be found by visiting the following websites:

blueletterbible.org   biblegateway.com   biblehub.com

MAIN POINTS	APPLY
Summarize the main point(s) or note any themes you encountered in the passage.	Apply God's Word specifically to your own life. Application is personal. God may teach, correct, rebuke, or train. He is always equipping. (II Tim. 3:16-17) Record what this passage means to you.

PRAY

Write a short prayer here. When we take time to write something down, that message becomes more etched on our heart. Take a moment to simply be with God. He is why we study. Savor. Know. Praise. Confess. Thank. Ask. Love. Then carry a nugget of His Word in your heart to ponder and proclaim throughout your day.

TO LIVE IS CHRIST,
AND TO DIE IS GAIN.

PHILIPPIANS 1:21

step by *step*

UNPACKING THE INDUCTIVE METHOD

step by *step*

UNPACKING THE INDUCTIVE METHOD

STEPS 1 & 2: READ AND OBSERVE | *See what the Bible **says***.
The first step to Bible study is simply reading God's Word.

The problem is that, in our hurried, scurried pace of life, we often plow right through it without taking time to ponder and think about what we're reading. *Observing* what we read helps us to slow down and take notice in order to see and answer, "What does the Bible *say*?"

Have you ever slowed down to truly examine and enjoy a piece of art? Artists have an amazing knack or ability to capture a particular scene, whether real or imagined, onto a blank canvas. How? Artists specialize in observing details. Setting, color, texture, time, characters, lighting, movement… the list of details is nearly limitless.

We can do this, too.

When they were young, blank sketch pads and new drawing pencils became a special treat for my children. Now imagine me with my small army of little ones traipsing off to a park with these tools in hand. Before pulling out a pencil to begin creating, the first thing to do was to find the right spot. (I highly recommend that for Bible study, too!) Then we'd observe.

To observe means "to see, watch, notice, or regard with attention, especially so as to see or learn something."[1] *Especially so as to see or learn something.*

And so, with my children, we would notice things. Lots of things! The different types of leaves, flowers, plants, grass, insects, animals, and more. Once engaged in observing, details begin to arise! How fun to zero in and observe the lady bug crawling along the

---

[1] **ethos**. Dictionary.com. *Dictionary.com Unabridged.* Random House, Inc. http://www.dictionary.com/browse/ethos (accessed: March 16, 2018).

blade of grass or the spots that adorn a toad sunning on the sidewalk or the veins that run throughout a maple leaf. There's so much to see!

Observation implies being curious. Noticing details. Asking questions.

Kids do this naturally. We can too. Be curious with God's Word. Scripture is full of details to notice and so many questions to ask. When we slow down to "smell the roses" within Scripture, we will see and learn something.

As you read, ask God's help to see what He would have you to see. Ask questions of the text and highlight verses that touch your heart. If anything is especially noteworthy to you, jot it down in the space to observe. (Keep in mind: this framework is simply a guide. You can fill in as little or as much of the space as you desire.)

The bottom line? Read. Read carefully. Then observe at least one thing. By doing so, we will see Scripture more clearly.

STEP 3: INTERPRET | *Understand what the Bible **means**.*

After careful observation of a landscape, an artist sketches an *interpretation* of what he sees onto the canvas. Observation and interpretation go hand in hand. A circle is a circle. A square is a square. As closely as possible, the artist defines and places an image of what he observes onto the canvas. Careful observation leads to a life-like rendering such that the viewer will enjoy a solid understanding of what the artist himself observed.

The same is true of the Bible. Observation and interpretation go hand in hand. Scripture will often interpret Scripture. As we carefully read and observe what the scripture says, we frequently understand and simultaneously interpret it's meaning. So, within our daily study format, observation and interpretation are located side-by-side.

One simple way to understand the meaning of Scripture is to answer any questions that we've asked of the text. Try answering them without the aid of study notes or other helps. Utilize scripture to interpret scripture.

Other times, interpretation is not so easy. After all, the Bible was written in ancient times, spanning the course of over 2,000 years, by a people and to a people of a culture that is utterly foreign to us.

Therefore, certain resources are handy. These tools help us to place and understand Scripture in its original context, in order to properly interpret what we've read. (Think of an artist pulling out a ruler—a simple tool that helps to more accurately reproduce a scene. A ruler is not necessary, but is useful.)

Bible study tools can include:

- *Cross references:* Cross references allow us to use nearby or related passages to more accurately interpret Scripture.
- *Bible dictionaries and concordances:* These tools allow us to understand the meaning of a word in its original language.
- *Bible handbooks and commentaries:* Resources like these help us to verify our conclusions as well as provide historical or cultural context.

It's important to remember that Scripture, in its original context, had only one meaning. Not multiple meanings. And although God can be mysterious, there are no mystical or hidden meanings within Scripture. Paul had a specific message, written at a specific time and in a specific place, for a specific group of people. He meant what he said. For this study, we want to know what Paul *meant* and how his audience *understood* him. Although we may not always be able to determine Paul's specific intent, that is our goal.

Interpretation implies understanding. Original meaning and context are important. Be reasonable. Compare.

Seek correct answers, but give yourself grace. A child's rendering of a ladybug on a blade of grass will not compare to Van Gogh's renderings, and yet, there is something wholly precious about the works of a child. Our renderings of Scripture won't ever equate to a Bible scholar's commentary. That's not our goal here. Our goal is knowing God. Sometimes this involves baby steps.

A, B, & C: TOOLS FOR INTERPRETATION

If the answers are not intuitive or easily found within the passage, tools are available to help us better understand. Our daily lesson format provides three boxes intended to support interpretation. Here, you'll find space to identify key words, define those key words, and record supporting vereses (cross references). These are intended to help and guide you as you interpret Scripture. Use them however you find them to be helpful.

> A. KEY WORDS: Did you notice that a word was repeated, seems important, is unfamiliar, or is interesting in any way? Record it here.
>
> B. DEFINITIONS: Use this box to record definitions of the key words you listed. For definitions, we have options:
>
> • *Read the verse using a different translation or version of the Bible.* This can be a very simple way to define a word. For example, our practice lesson (on page 22) notes the word **apostle** from I Timothy 1:1. The ESV translation says "apostle," while the Amplified Bible expounds: "apostle (special messenger, personally chosen representative)." [1]
>
> • *Use a Bible concordance.* My favorite way to define a word is to use a concordance. This tool looks at words in their original language. I like the **Strong's Concordance**, which can also be found online.
>
> > **i.** Going online? Try **Blue Letter Bible**, a free web-based concordance.
> >
> > **ii.** Once there, (referring to our practice lesson on page 22) simply type "I Timothy 1" into the "Search the Bible" box. Click on the box

---

[1] The Holy Bible: The Amplified Bible. 1987. La Habra, CA: The Lockman Foundation.

called **TOOLS** next to I Timothy 1:1 and an assortment of choices will arrive. Find the corresponding Strong's Concordance number for "apostle" (in this case: G652) and click on it. You'll retrieve the Greek word, original definitions, and how it is used in other places of the Bible. It's fascinating! Make note of the definitions you find.

- *Try a Bible dictionary.* In order to define people or find places, Bible dictionaries are handy.

    i. Online, you can try **Bible Gateway, Blue Letter Bible,** or **Bible Hub** for free.

    ii. There are also wonderful apps available for you to use. A friend recently introduced me to **Bible Map.** This app is simple to use and automatically syncs Scripture with maps.

C. CROSS REFERENCES: Some Bibles offer cross references. This is a solid way to allow Scripture to interpret Scripture. Perhaps your Bible does not include cross references (most journaling Bibles do not). No worries! It's very easy to access cross references online. **Bible Hub** is a great place to start!

Your daily lesson framework also offers space for you to identify the main point of the passage you've read. Here, you may summarize the main point(s) or any recurring themes you noticed in the passage. Understanding the main idea always helps us to interpret a scenario correctly.

WANTING EVEN MORE? Our daily study format includes space for key words, definitions, and cross references, along with space to identify the main points of the passage you're studying. However, there are other helps available if you'd like to dig deeper. Biblical commentaries are books written by Biblical scholars. Commentaries often provide solid cultural and historical context while commenting verse-by-verse on Scripture.

Personally, I admire the dedication and genius of the scholars who write commentaries. These amazingly dedicated scholars study for the glory of God. And yet, it's best to save these resources for last. Why? Because commentaries are not a substitute for reading and understanding God's Word on your own. Seek to understand on your own first.

Also, please note that commentaries are often written according to various theological bents. It's helpful to compare. Know your sources. This is especially crucial if roaming the Internet. Please surf with discernment and great care.

Still not satisfied? Note your question and talk to God about it. Ponder. Many times, as you ponder a verse, God will interpret. Other times, He allows certain things to remain a mystery. He is sovereign. We walk by faith.

Remember to share and discuss your questions with others at Bible study, either in person or online. Studying God's Word is meant to be done in community. We encourage, learn, and grow together.

Finally, check out our website: **www.simplybible.study**.

STEP 4: APPLICATION | *Put it all **together**.*

With the Holy Spirit's illumination, careful observation, and good interpretation, we better understand the meaning of a passage. And that's thrilling! Oftentimes, finding a nugget of truth, a promise, or a revelation about God Himself takes my breath away! There is no other book like it:

> For the word of God is living and active, sharper than any two-edged sword, piercing to the division of soul and of spirit, of joints and of marrow, and discerning the thoughts and intentions of the heart.
> *Hebrews 4:12*

The God of the Universe loves us and personally reveals Himself through His Living Word. When He does, it cuts in a good way. Then we're ready to *apply* His Word to our everyday lives.

Application is the fun and creative part. Yes, the original author of Scripture had one meaning, but the personal applications of Scripture are many. This part is between you and God. A particular verse, word, or idea might strike a chord in your heart. Slow down. Take note. Show God the discovery. This is the amazing process of God revealing Himself and His truth to you through His Word and the power of His Holy Spirit.

God looks at our hearts. He sees, knows, and loves His sheep. And so, He may use His Word to teach, correct, rebuke, or train. He is always equipping. (II Timothy 3:16-17) If you're willing, He will lead you to apply His Word specifically to your everyday life.

Application ideas include:
1. Worship God for who He is, according to a truth or promised discovered.
2. Thank Him for a lesson learned.
3. Note an example to follow.
4. Confess a sin revealed.
5. Pray a prayer noticed.
6. Obey, trust, and follow God's way, His command, His plan.
7. Memorize a verse.

WRAPPING UP: PRAYER | *Respond to a **holy** God.*

Application implies a recognition of who God is. And so, wrapping up personal study with application nearly always leads me to bow down in worship, at least bowing my heart. Hence, the **SIMPLY BIBLE** daily format includes a place for *prayer*. Please use this! It may be the most important space of all.

Enjoy being together with Him in His Word. Savor. Learn. Grow. Know. Thank. Praise. Love. Then carry a nugget of truth in your heart to ponder with Him as you go about your day.

lesson *samples*

PRACTICE LESSONS & EXAMPLES

practice *lesson*
A STEP-BY-STEP GUIDE

Below are two verses, I Timothy 1:1-2. As you read, feel free to highlight, circle, underline and mark up the text in whatever way you like. In the *Observe* column, jot down details that pop out and write down questions that come to mind. Then interpret. Simply use the Scripture itself or hop over to boxes A, B, and C to define a word or find a cross reference that will help you better understand.

Finish by summarizing, applying, and praying.

This is *your* workbook. It is meant to be a journal of your thoughts as you engage with God and His Word. Don't be shy. Be you, be with God, and enjoy!

READ	OBSERVE	INTERPRET
¹ Paul, an apostle of Christ Jesus by command of God our Savior and of Christ Jesus our hope, ² To Timothy, my true child in the faith: Grace, mercy, and peace from God the Father and Christ Jesus our Lord.		

KEY WORDS	DEFINITIONS	CROSS REFERENCES

MAIN POINT(S)	APPLY

PRAY

sample *lesson*

1 TIMOTHY 1:1-2 | FOR THOSE CRAZY, BUSY DAYS

Life gets hectic. We get busy. It happens. Some days, you just don't have the time to go very deep in your study. That's okay! But even reading just a few verses and aiming to hone in on *one* important detail is better than nothing at all! Here's what it might look like to observe, interpret, and apply just *one* thing:

READ	OBSERVE	INTERPRET
¹ Paul, an apostle of Christ Jesus by command of God our Savior and of Christ Jesus our hope, ² To Timothy, my true child in the faith: Grace, mercy, and peace from God the Father and Christ Jesus our Lord.	Christ Jesus is mentioned 3 times. According to Paul, who is he?	Jesus is "our hope." He is "our Lord." He commanded Paul to be His apostle. He gives grace, mercy, and peace.

KEY WORDS	DEFINITIONS	CROSS REFERENCES
apostle	a special messenger, a personally-chosen representative (Amplified Bible)	I Timothy 1:12 I thank him who has given me strength, Christ Jesus our Lord, because he judged me faithful, appointing me to his service...

MAIN POINT(S)

The apostle Paul greets Timothy in a letter.

APPLY

Even in a greeting of a letter, Paul brings glory to Jesus and reminds Timothy of the hope we have in Him. How can I greet others with this same exuberance for Christ throughout my day today?

PRAY

Lord God, thank You for today's reminder of hope. I praise You, Jesus, for **you are Lord.** And You are the giver of grace, mercy, and peace. Thank You! Like Paul, may I be a vessel of Your hope, grace, mercy, and peace today.

sample *lesson*

1 TIMOTHY 1:1-2 | GOING DEEPER

On occasion, you may find yourself wanting to go a little deeper in your study. Here's an example of what that could look like. You can observe as much or as little as you like. Remember: no two journals will look the same.

READ	OBSERVE	INTERPRET
¹ Paul, an apostle of Christ Jesus by command of God our Savior and of Christ Jesus our hope, ² To Timothy, my true child in the faith: Grace, mercy, and peace from God the Father and Christ Jesus our Lord.	Who is Paul? What is an apostle? Christ Jesus is mentioned 3 times in two verses! Who is He? Why is He our hope? Who is Timothy? Paul refers to Timothy as "my" true child. Why? Faith in what? Is it common to offer grace, mercy, and peace in a greeting? Notice Paul distinguishes between God the Father and Jesus Christ.	Paul: an apostle of Jesus. Apostle: chosen by God Jesus is our hope and our Lord. He commanded Paul to be His apostle. He gives grace, mercy, and peace. Christ is our Savior. He is also "in us." (Col.1:27) Timothy: Paul's "true child in the faith." Not sure why Paul uses this phrase. Perhaps Paul witnessed to Timothy and was a part of his spiritual "birth." Faith: Belief in Christ. Mercy is found in other greetings: II Timothy 1, 2 John 3, Jude 2, but overall is unique for Paul to include in his letters.

KEY WORDS	DEFINITIONS	CROSS REFERENCES
apostle	a special messenger, a personally-chosen representative (Amplified Bible)	**I Timothy 1:12** - I thank him who has given me strength, Christ Jesus our Lord, because he judged me faithful, appointing me to his service...
hope	an expectation	**Colossians 1:27** - To them God chose to make known how great among the Gentiles are the riches of the glory of this mystery, which is Christ in you, the hope of glory.
true child in the faith		**Titus 1:4** - To Titus, my true child in a common faith...

MAIN POINT(S)

The apostle Paul greets Timothy in a letter.

APPLY

Even in a greeting, Paul brings glory to Jesus and reminds Timothy of the hope we have in Him. How can I greet others with this same exuberance for Christ? What am I doing to "give birth" to children of the faith? Praise God for His grace, peace, and mercy! Am I extending this to others?

PRAY

Lord God, thank You for today's reminder of hope. I praise You, Jesus, for **you are Lord.** And You are the giver of grace, mercy, and peace. Thank You! Like Paul, may I be a vessel of Your hope, grace, mercy, and peace today. Lord, I pray for open doors to share Christ with _____. Please prepare her heart to receive your grace and peace.

YOU DID IT! That's it. That's all there is to it. If this is your first time, perhaps the process felt awkward. Don't worry. You probably don't remember how clumsy and time-consuming it was the very first time you tried tying your shoe, riding a bike, or driving a car. Practice helps. Same for Bible study.

You're more observant, smarter, and stronger than you think you are. God created you that way. More importantly, He is with you. His desire is to be known. Lean into Him. Ask, seek, and you will find. His grace is sufficient. His power is made perfect in our weakness.

> For as the rain and the snow come down from heaven
> > and do not return there but water the earth,
> making it bring forth and sprout,
> > giving seed to the sower and bread to the eater,
> so shall my word be that goes out from my mouth;
> > it shall not return to me empty,
> but it shall accomplish that which I purpose,
> > and shall succeed in the thing for which I sent it.
> For you shall go out in joy
> > and be led forth in peace;
> the mountains and the hills before you
> > shall break forth into singing,
> > and all the trees of the field shall clap their hands.
>
> Isaiah 55:10-12

Lord God Almighty, thank You for Your Word! Like rain and snow watering the earth so that it might bud and flourish, may Your Word now water our hearts, minds, and souls to flourish in our love for You and for one another. May Your purposes and desires be accomplished. As we study with You, may we go out in joy and be led forth in Your peace. With all creation may we sing and clap for joy and bring glory to Your Name...

in *context*

EXAMINING THE CONTEXT OF PHILIPPIANS

CHRIST IS PROCLAIMED,
AND IN THAT I REJOICE.

PHILIPPIANS 1:18

in *context*

EXAMINING THE CONTEXT OF PHILIPPIANS

PHILIPPIANS: A letter written by the Apostle Paul to the church in Philippi, located in Macedonia. Differing from Ephesus, a great city because of its bustling commerce and religion, Philippi's importance stemmed from its status as a Roman city and a hub for the Roman government in Asia. Philippi prospered because it reigned over a significant amount of territory and was granted legal status as a Roman colony. Here, the colonists possessed full Roman citizenship. Benefits of citizenship included exemption from paying certain taxes. The law and judicial system were Roman.

As recorded by Luke in Acts 16, Paul and Silas headed to Macedonia following Paul's vision of a Macedonian man calling to him for help. Paul's first convert in Philippi was a woman named Lydia, a dealer in purple cloth from Thyatira. She and her household were baptized, and a small church was born. While ministering in Philippi, both Paul and Silas were beaten, publically disgraced, and cast into prison after exorcising a spirit from a slave girl and angering her owners. Paul mentions this "outrageous" incident in I Thessalonians 2:2.

The style of Paul's letter to the Philippians is endearing and thankful. Paul writes from prison and is filled with joy as he remembers his friends and gives thanks for their care and generosity to him. The Philippians have partnered with him since the beginning (1:5). This letter communicates both friendship and encouragement. In Pauline style, while expressing his gratitude, he also snatches the opportunity to encourage believers.

Paul's desire? That the "manner of their lives be worthy of the gospel of Christ" (1:27). He calls believers to unity, to be of one mind, and specifically, to have the mind of Christ. Themes of joy in the midst of suffering reign throughout this epistle. Paul himself models contentment. Friendly and encouraging, Philippians reveals Paul's recipe for a joyful, contented, and grateful heart.

the roman *empire*

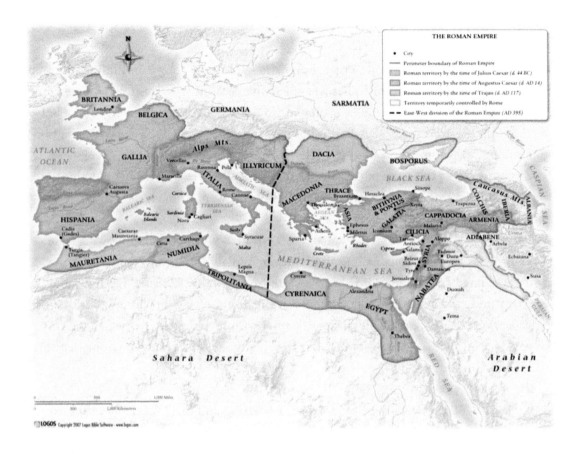

---

[1] Map provided by Logos Bible Software.

keeping *time*

A TIMELINE OF PAUL'S JOURNEY

- 28 — Jesus' public ministry begins (28-30)
- 30 — Jesus' crucifixion
- 32 —
- Paul's conversion
- 34 —
- Paul's first post-conversion Jerusalem visit
- 36 — Paul in Cilicia and Syria (35-46)
- 38 —
- 40 —
- 42 —
- 44 —
- 46 — Paul's second Jerusalem visit
- Paul and Barnabus in Cyprus and Galatia
- 48 — *Paul writes his letter to the Galatians (?)*
- Council of Jerusalem
- 50 — Paul & Silas travel from Syrian Antioch to Macedonia and Achaia (49-50)
- *Paul writes his letter to the Thessalonians*
- 52 — Paul in Corinth (50-52); Paul's third Jerusalem visit
- Paul in Ephesus (52-55)
- 54 —
- *Paul writes his letters to the Corinthians (55-56)*
- 56 — Paul in Macedonia, Illyricum, and Achaia
- *Paul writes his letter to the Romans;* Paul's final Jerusalem visit
- 58 — Paul's imprisonment in Caesarea (57-59)
- Paul's voyage to Rome begins
- 60 — Paul arrives in Rome
- Paul placed under house-arrest in Rome (60-62)
- 62 — *Paul writes his "captivity letters" (60-62?)*
- 64 —

---

[1] Bruce, F. F. (2000). *Paul, Apostle of the Heart Set Free*. Cumbria, UK: Paternoster Press.

HE WHO BEGAN A GOOD
WORK IN YOU WILL BRING
IT TO COMPLETION AT THE
DAY OF JESUS CHRIST.

PHILIPPIANS 1:6

live *joyfully*

BECOMING A **DOER** OF THE WORD

> CHRIST WILL BE HONORED IN MY BODY, WHETHER BY LIFE OR BY DEATH.
>
> PHILIPPIANS 1:20

the 28 days of joy *challenge*
BECOMING A **DOER** OF THE WORD

Joy is an attribute of the Spirit that can grow through praise, thanksgiving, and trusting and obeying God. As we embark on this study, let's seek to be mindful of the ways that we can find joy in Jesus. Each day, record a praise to God, give Him thanks, OR write down a specific way that you are choosing to trust and obey Him. For a triple threat against anxious thoughts, try all three!

> Rejoice in the Lord always; again I will say, rejoice. Let your reasonableness be known to everyone. The Lord is at hand; do not be anxious about anything, but in everything by prayer and supplication with thanksgiving let your requests be made known to God. And the peace of God, which surpasses all understanding, will guard your hearts and your minds in Christ Jesus.
> *Philippians 4:4-7*

	PRAISE	THANKSGIVING	TRUST & OBEY
S			
M			
T			
W			
T			
F			
S			

	PRAISE	THANKSGIVING	TRUST & OBEY
S			
M			
T			
W			
T			
F			
S			

	PRAISE	THANKSGIVING	TRUST & OBEY
S			
M			
T			
W			
T			
F			
S			

	PRAISE	THANKSGIVING	TRUST & OBEY
S			
M			
T			
W			
T			
F			
S			

chapter *one*

PHILIPPIANS

take *note*

NOTES ON PHILIPPIANS 1

take *note*

NOTES ON PHILIPPIANS 1

day *one*

PHILIPPIANS 1:1-11

READ	OBSERVE	INTERPRET
¹ Paul and Timothy, servants of Christ Jesus, To all the saints in Christ Jesus who are at Philippi, with the overseers and deacons: ² Grace to you and peace from God our Father and the Lord Jesus Christ. ³ I thank my God in all my remembrance of you, ⁴ always in every prayer of mine for you all making my prayer with joy, ⁵ because of your partnership in the gospel from the first day until now. ⁶ And I am sure of this, that he who began a good work in you will bring it to completion at the day of Jesus Christ. ⁷ It is right for me to feel this way about you all, because I hold you in my heart, for you are all partakers with me of grace, both in my imprisonment and in the defense and confirmation of the gospel. ⁸ For God is my witness, how I yearn for you all with the affection of Christ Jesus. ⁹ And it is my prayer that your love may abound more and more, with knowledge and all discernment, ¹⁰ so that you may approve what is excellent, and so be pure and blameless for the day of Christ, ¹¹ filled with the fruit of righteousness that comes through Jesus Christ, to the glory and praise of God.		

KEY WORDS	DEFINITIONS	CROSS REFERENCES

MAIN POINT(S)	APPLY

PRAY

day *two*

PHILIPPIANS 1:12-18

READ	OBSERVE	INTERPRET
¹² I want you to know, brothers, that what has happened to me has really served to advance the gospel, ¹³ so that it has become known throughout the whole imperial guard and to all the rest that my imprisonment is for Christ. ¹⁴ And most of the brothers, having become confident in the Lord by my imprisonment, are much more bold to speak the word without fear. ¹⁵ Some indeed preach Christ from envy and rivalry, but others from good will. ¹⁶ The latter do it out of love, knowing that I am put here for the defense of the gospel. ¹⁷ The former proclaim Christ out of selfish ambition, not sincerely but thinking to afflict me in my imprisonment. ¹⁸ What then? Only that in every way, whether in pretense or in truth, Christ is proclaimed, and in that I rejoice.		

| KEY WORDS | DEFINITIONS | CROSS REFERENCES |
|---|---|---|ита
| | | |

MAIN POINT(S)	APPLY

PRAY

day *three*

PHILIPPIANS 1:19-26

READ	OBSERVE	INTERPRET
Yes, and I will rejoice, ¹⁹ for I know that through your prayers and the help of the Spirit of Jesus Christ this will turn out for my deliverance, ²⁰ as it is my eager expectation and hope that I will not be at all ashamed, but that with full courage now as always Christ will be honored in my body, whether by life or by death. ²¹ For to me to live is Christ, and to die is gain. ²² If I am to live in the flesh, that means fruitful labor for me. Yet which I shall choose I cannot tell. ²³ I am hard pressed between the two. My desire is to depart and be with Christ, for that is far better. ²⁴ But to remain in the flesh is more necessary on your account. ²⁵ Convinced of this, I know that I will remain and continue with you all, for your progress and joy in the faith, ²⁶ so that in me you may have ample cause to glory in Christ Jesus, because of my coming to you again.		

KEY WORDS	DEFINITIONS	CROSS REFERENCES

MAIN POINT(S)	APPLY

PRAY

day *four*

PHILIPPIANS 1:27-30

READ	OBSERVE	INTERPRET
²⁷ Only let your manner of life be worthy of the gospel of Christ, so that whether I come and see you or am absent, I may hear of you that you are standing firm in one spirit, with one mind striving side by side for the faith of the gospel, ²⁸ and not frightened in anything by your opponents. This is a clear sign to them of their destruction, but of your salvation, and that from God. ²⁹ For it has been granted to you that for the sake of Christ you should not only believe in him but also suffer for his sake, ³⁰ engaged in the same conflict that you saw I had and now hear that I still have.		

| KEY WORDS | DEFINITIONS | CROSS REFERENCES |

| MAIN POINT(S) | APPLY |

PRAY

day *five*

PHILIPPIANS 1 | REVIEW & DISCUSSION QUESTIONS

1 Summary:	2 Write out a favorite verse(s) from the passage, perhaps in your own words:
3 Why is Paul thankful and always praying with joy for the Philippians?	4 Explain the difference between joy and happiness.
5 Define *partnership* (1:5). Does this differ from modern ideas of church "fellowship?" How are you partnering with others to advance the gospel?	6 What are Paul's specific prayer requests on behalf of the Philippians (1:9-11)?

7 What has happened to Paul, and how has this "served the advance of the Gospel" (1:12-14)?

8 Share your thoughts concerning Paul's attitude about his present circumstances (1:18).

9 In verse 21, Paul says, "to live is Christ and to die is gain." How is Christ glorified if Paul lives? If he dies?

10 How is Paul a role model? Can Christ be glorified through a difficult circumstance in your own life today? Explain.

11 What does Paul mean when he says, "let your manner of life be worthy of the gospel of Christ" (1:27)?

12 Praise God for at least one truth from this week's study:

take it to *heart*

USE THIS SPACE TO WRITE OUT OR JOURNAL A FAVORITE VERSE OR PASSAGE FROM THIS WEEK'S STUDY

chapter *two*

PHILIPPIANS

take *note*

NOTES ON PHILIPPIANS 2

take *note*

NOTES ON PHILIPPIANS 2

day *one*

PHILIPPIANS 2:1-4

READ	OBSERVE	INTERPRET
¹ So if there is any encouragement in Christ, any comfort from love, any participation in the Spirit, any affection and sympathy, ² complete my joy by being of the same mind, having the same love, being in full accord and of one mind. ³ Do nothing from selfish ambition or conceit, but in humility count others more significant than yourselves. ⁴ Let each of you look not only to his own interests, but also to the interests of others.		

KEY WORDS	DEFINITIONS	CROSS REFERENCES

MAIN POINT(S)	APPLY

PRAY

day *two*

PHILIPPIANS 2:5-11

READ	OBSERVE	INTERPRET
⁵ Have this mind among yourselves, which is yours in Christ Jesus, ⁶ who, though he was in the form of God, did not count equality with God a thing to be grasped, ⁷ but emptied himself, by taking the form of a servant, being born in the likeness of men. ⁸ And being found in human form, he humbled himself by becoming obedient to the point of death, even death on a cross. ⁹ Therefore God has highly exalted him and bestowed on him the name that is above every name, ¹⁰ so that at the name of Jesus every knee should bow, in heaven and on earth and under the earth, ¹¹ and every tongue confess that Jesus Christ is Lord, to the glory of God the Father.		

| KEY WORDS | DEFINITIONS | CROSS REFERENCES |

| MAIN POINT(S) | APPLY |

PRAY

day *three*

PHILIPPIANS 2:12-18

READ	OBSERVE	INTERPRET
¹² Therefore, my beloved, as you have always obeyed, so now, not only as in my presence but much more in my absence, work out your own salvation with fear and trembling, ¹³ for it is God who works in you, both to will and to work for his good pleasure. ¹⁴ Do all things without grumbling or disputing, ¹⁵ that you may be blameless and innocent, children of God without blemish in the midst of a crooked and twisted generation, among whom you shine as lights in the world, ¹⁶ holding fast to the word of life, so that in the day of Christ I may be proud that I did not run in vain or labor in vain. ¹⁷ Even if I am to be poured out as a drink offering upon the sacrificial offering of your faith, I am glad and rejoice with you all. ¹⁸ Likewise you also should be glad and rejoice with me.		

| KEY WORDS | DEFINITIONS | CROSS REFERENCES |

| MAIN POINT(S) | APPLY |

PRAY

day *four*

PHILIPPIANS 2:19-30

READ

¹⁹ I hope in the Lord Jesus to send Timothy to you soon, so that I too may be cheered by news of you. ²⁰ For I have no one like him, who will be genuinely concerned for your welfare. ²¹ For they all seek their own interests, not those of Jesus Christ. ²² But you know Timothy's proven worth, how as a son with a father he has served with me in the gospel. ²³ I hope therefore to send him just as soon as I see how it will go with me, ²⁴ and I trust in the Lord that shortly I myself will come also.

²⁵ I have thought it necessary to send to you Epaphroditus my brother and fellow worker and fellow soldier, and your messenger and minister to my need, ²⁶ for he has been longing for you all and has been distressed because you heard that he was ill. ²⁷ Indeed he was ill, near to death. But God had mercy on him, and not only on him but on me also, lest I should have sorrow upon sorrow. ²⁸ I am the more eager to send him, therefore, that you may rejoice at seeing him again, and that I may be less anxious. ²⁹ So receive him in the Lord with all joy, and honor such men, ³⁰ for he nearly died for the work of Christ, risking his life to complete what was lacking in your service to me.

OBSERVE

INTERPRET

| KEY WORDS | DEFINITIONS | CROSS REFERENCES |

| MAIN POINT(S) | APPLY |

PRAY

day *five*

PHILIPPIANS 2 | REVIEW & DISCUSSION QUESTIONS

1 Summary:	2 Write out a favorite verse(s) from the passage, perhaps in your own words:
3 In what ways can the Philippians "complete" Paul's joy" (2:2)?	4 What attitude are we to have (2:5)? Describe.
5 Why is humility important? How can you develop this quality?	6 Ponder verses 9-11. What are practical ways to acknowledge Christ's Lordship today?

7 In what way are the Philippians to "work out" their salvation (2:12-15)?

8 **True or False:** *I "do all things without grumbling or disputing."* What specific area of life most challenges you in this way? Explain.

9 What benefit comes from doing all things without grumbling or disputing (2:14-16)?

10 How does Paul describe Timothy's importance (2:19-24)? How can you be a Timothy to someone else?

11 What commendation does Paul give to Epaphroditus (2:25-30)?

12 Praise God for at least one truth from this week's study:

take it to *heart*

USE THIS SPACE TO WRITE OUT OR JOURNAL A FAVORITE VERSE OR PASSAGE FROM THIS WEEK'S STUDY

IT IS GOD WHO WORKS IN YOU, BOTH TO WILL AND TO WORK FOR HIS GOOD PLEASURE.

PHILIPPIANS 2:13

chapter *three*
PHILIPPIANS

take *note*

NOTES ON PHILIPPIANS 3

take *note*

NOTES ON PHILIPPIANS 3

day *one*

PHILIPPIANS 3:1-6

READ	OBSERVE	INTERPRET
¹ Finally, my brothers, rejoice in the Lord. To write the same things to you is no trouble to me and is safe for you. ² Look out for the dogs, look out for the evildoers, look out for those who mutilate the flesh. ³ For we are the circumcision, who worship by the Spirit of God and glory in Christ Jesus and put no confidence in the flesh— ⁴ though I myself have reason for confidence in the flesh also. If anyone else thinks he has reason for confidence in the flesh, I have more: ⁵ circumcised on the eighth day, of the people of Israel, of the tribe of Benjamin, a Hebrew of Hebrews; as to the law, a Pharisee; ⁶ as to zeal, a persecutor of the church; as to righteousness under the law, blameless.		

KEY WORDS	DEFINITIONS	CROSS REFERENCES

MAIN POINT(S)	APPLY

PRAY

day *two*

PHILIPPIANS 3:7-11

READ	OBSERVE	INTERPRET
⁷ But whatever gain I had, I counted as loss for the sake of Christ. ⁸ Indeed, I count everything as loss because of the surpassing worth of knowing Christ Jesus my Lord. For his sake I have suffered the loss of all things and count them as rubbish, in order that I may gain Christ ⁹ and be found in him, not having a righteousness of my own that comes from the law, but that which comes through faith in Christ, the righteousness from God that depends on faith— ¹⁰ that I may know him and the power of his resurrection, and may share his sufferings, becoming like him in his death, ¹¹ that by any means possible I may attain the resurrection from the dead.		

KEY WORDS	**DEFINITIONS**	**CROSS REFERENCES**

MAIN POINT(S)	**APPLY**

PRAY

day *three*

PHILIPPIANS 3:12-16

READ	OBSERVE	INTERPRET
¹² Not that I have already obtained this or am already perfect, but I press on to make it my own, because Christ Jesus has made me his own. ¹³ Brothers, I do not consider that I have made it my own. But one thing I do: forgetting what lies behind and straining forward to what lies ahead, ¹⁴ I press on toward the goal for the prize of the upward call of God in Christ Jesus. ¹⁵ Let those of us who are mature think this way, and if in anything you think otherwise, God will reveal that also to you. ¹⁶ Only let us hold true to what we have attained.		

KEY WORDS	DEFINITIONS	CROSS REFERENCES

MAIN POINT(S)	APPLY

PRAY

day *four*

PHILIPPIANS 3:17-21

READ	OBSERVE	INTERPRET
¹⁷ Brothers, join in imitating me, and keep your eyes on those who walk according to the example you have in us. ¹⁸ For many, of whom I have often told you and now tell you even with tears, walk as enemies of the cross of Christ. ¹⁹ Their end is destruction, their god is their belly, and they glory in their shame, with minds set on earthly things. ²⁰ But our citizenship is in heaven, and from it we await a Savior, the Lord Jesus Christ, ²¹ who will transform our lowly body to be like his glorious body, by the power that enables him even to subject all things to himself.		

KEY WORDS	DEFINITIONS	CROSS REFERENCES

MAIN POINT(S)	APPLY

PRAY

day *five*

PHILIPPIANS 3 | REVIEW & DISCUSSION QUESTIONS

1 Summary:	2 Write out a favorite verse(s) from the passage, perhaps in your own words:
3 In verse 1, Paul says, "Rejoice in the Lord." Practically, what does this look like?	4 What warning does Paul give in verse 2? Explain.
5 List Paul's "fleshly" credentials (3:5-6). What value does he place on these (3:7-9)?	6 What credentials do you hold up in high esteem? By what credentials are we measured in God's kingdom?

7 Explain what Paul means to "be found in Christ" (3:9). Are you "in Christ?" When and how did that happen?	8 What is the benefit of "forgetting what is behind and straining toward what is ahead" (3:13)? Is there something you need to "forget" in order to move "ahead?"
9 Why does Paul "press on?" What's his goal? How do your goals compare?	10 What is the motivation of the "false apostles" to whom Paul refers in verses 18-19?
11 What benefits come with "citizenship" of a country? Is there a correlation to our heavenly citizenship? Explain.	12 Praise God for at least one truth from this week's study:

take it to *heart*

USE THIS SPACE TO WRITE OUT OR JOURNAL A FAVORITE VERSE OR PASSAGE FROM THIS WEEK'S STUDY

chapter *four*

PHILIPPIANS

take *note*

NOTES ON PHILIPPIANS 4

take *note*

NOTES ON PHILIPPIANS 4

day *one*

PHILIPPIANS 4:1-3

READ	OBSERVE	INTERPRET
¹ Therefore, my brothers, whom I love and long for, my joy and crown, stand firm thus in the Lord, my beloved. ² I entreat Euodia and I entreat Syntyche to agree in the Lord. ³ Yes, I ask you also, true companion, help these women, who have labored side by side with me in the gospel together with Clement and the rest of my fellow workers, whose names are in the book of life.		

| KEY WORDS | DEFINITIONS | CROSS REFERENCES |

| MAIN POINT(S) | APPLY |

PRAY

day *two*

PHILIPPIANS 4:4-9

READ

For today's reading, please look up the passage in your own Bible and hand-write the verses here.

OBSERVE

INTERPRET

KEY WORDS	DEFINITIONS	CROSS REFERENCES

MAIN POINT(S)	APPLY

PRAY

day *three*

PHILIPPIANS 4:10-19

READ	OBSERVE	INTERPRET
¹⁰ I rejoiced in the Lord greatly that now at length you have revived your concern for me. You were indeed concerned for me, but you had no opportunity. ¹¹ Not that I am speaking of being in need, for I have learned in whatever situation I am to be content. ¹² I know how to be brought low, and I know how to abound. In any and every circumstance, I have learned the secret of facing plenty and hunger, abundance and need. ¹³ I can do all things through him who strengthens me. ¹⁴ Yet it was kind of you to share my trouble. ¹⁵ And you Philippians yourselves know that in the beginning of the gospel, when I left Macedonia, no church entered into partnership with me in giving and receiving, except you only. ¹⁶ Even in Thessalonica you sent me help for my needs once and again. ¹⁷ Not that I seek the gift, but I seek the fruit that increases to your credit. ¹⁸ I have received full payment, and more. I am well supplied, having received from Epaphroditus the gifts you sent, a fragrant offering, a sacrifice acceptable and pleasing to God. ¹⁹ And my God will supply every need of yours according to his riches in glory in Christ Jesus.		

KEY WORDS	DEFINITIONS	CROSS REFERENCES

MAIN POINT(S)	APPLY

PRAY

day *four*

PHILIPPIANS 4:20-23

READ	OBSERVE	INTERPRET
²⁰ To our God and Father be glory forever and ever. Amen. ²¹ Greet every saint in Christ Jesus. The brothers who are with me greet you. ²² All the saints greet you, especially those of Caesar's household. ²³ The grace of the Lord Jesus Christ be with your spirit.		

KEY WORDS	DEFINITIONS	CROSS REFERENCES

MAIN POINT(S)	APPLY

PRAY

day *five*

PHILIPPIANS 4 | REVIEW & DISCUSSION QUESTIONS

1 Summary:	2 Write out a favorite verse(s) from the passage, perhaps in your own words:
3 Describe what Paul means when he exhorts the Philippians to "stand firm" in verse 1.	4 Verses 2 and 3 hint at disunity between two women of the church. Why is unity so important?
5 How do we "rejoice in the Lord always?"	6 Are there specific ways you struggle with anxious thoughts?

7 Describe Paul's antidote for dealing with anxiety (4:4-8).

8 Do Paul's words have implications for how you spend time? Explain.

9 What has Paul learned of contentment? How does this inspire you?

10 From verses 14-18, how would you describe the Philippians? What are the benefits of giving?

11 What do you learn of Paul's faith from verse 19? How does your own faith compare? Is there a current need for which you're having difficulty trusting God?

12 Praise God for at least one truth from this week's study:

take it to *heart*

USE THIS SPACE TO WRITE OUT OR JOURNAL A FAVORITE VERSE OR PASSAGE FROM THIS WEEK'S STUDY

final *thoughts*
WRAPPING UP

final *thoughts*

THE BOOK OF PHILIPPIANS | WRAPPING UP

1 Choose your favorite verse from Philippians. Write it out here. Give an explanation of what this verse means to you or why you find it impactful.

2 Consider the book of Philippians as a whole. What overarching themes did you notice within this book throughout your study?

3 How would you summarize the book of Philippians in a single word?

4 Praise God for a truth that He has revealed to you or for a way that He has worked in your life as a result of your study of Philippians:

pause and *reflect*

USE THIS SPACE TO WRITE OUT A PRAYER, A KEY PASSAGE, OR A REFLECTION ON YOUR STUDY OF PHILIPPIANS

leader *guide*

MAXIMIZING THE SMALL-GROUP EXPERIENCE

GO THEREFORE AND MAKE DISCIPLES OF ALL NATIONS, BAPTIZING THEM IN THE NAME OF THE FATHER AND OF THE SON AND OF THE HOLY SPIRIT, TEACHING THEM TO OBSERVE ALL THAT I HAVE COMMANDED YOU.

MATTHEW 28:19-20

introduction

LEADING WOMEN THROUGH **SIMPLY BIBLE**

Welcome to **SIMPLY BIBLE**, and thank you for your commitment to walk alongside a group of women for this season of exploring God's Word. In my own life, God has proven Himself faithful. Time and again as I lead women and seek to be a blessing to others, the blessing always seems to be mine. He is gracious that way. So, it is my heartfelt prayer for leaders that, as you seek to be a blessing to others, you too will be blessed beyond measure by the experience of shepherding women through God's Word. Truly, what a privilege it is to facilitate conversations that point women to Christ!

The primary objective of **SIMPLY BIBLE** is this:

> To inspire every woman to love God with all her heart, soul, mind, and strength, and to love others as herself. (Luke 10:27)

And *you*, the small-group leader, will play an important role in inspiring women to do exactly that! You will lead your group through meaningful conversations, with the help of the discussion questions found at the end of every chapter in this workbook. Our intention here is to help women grow in their relationships with Jesus Christ. It is also my hope that you will connect with the women in your groups on a personal level, gently guiding them to authentic relationships with one another.

guarding your *heart*
LEADING FROM THE RIGHT PERSPECTIVE

Ethos is a Latin word that denotes the fundamental character or spirit of a community, group, or person. When used to discuss dramatic literature, ethos is that moral element used to determine a character's action rather than his or her thought or emotion. Ethos points to the inward being, to the moral fabric of the heart. In Biblical language, ethos absolutely compares to a person's heart. And our ethos, our heart, is important to God.

His Word tells us:

> Above all else, guard your heart,
> for everything you do flows from it.
> Proverbs 4:23 NIV

Above all else, guard your heart. Why? Because everything we do flows from the heart, from our inward being. And that "everything" includes leading women through God's Word. If we want to see women growing in authentic relationships with Christ and with one another, that process must first begin in our own hearts.

> For the Lord sees not as man sees: man looks on the
> outward appearance, but the Lord looks on the heart.
> I Samuel 16:7

So often, as individuals and as women's ministry groups, we get caught up in appearances. I'm guilty. How easy it is for us as leaders to dress ourselves up for Bible study, look nice on the outside, make sure the tables are inviting, share a few pleasant words, all the while never touching the core or the heart in order to make heart connections with God and with one another. God looks at the heart. Perhaps we should, too.

Truly, I believe that I could write a book concerning effectively "guarding our hearts" while leading women in inductive Bible study. However, for our purposes today, let's keep things simple and limit our necessary ingredients to three:

(1) Jesus
(2) Prayer
(3) The Word

By guarding our hearts in these ways, successful Bible study leadership is certain. Let's briefly understand.

GUARDING YOUR HEART WITH JESUS

This may seem so obvious, but honestly, isn't it easy for us to miss the forest for the trees? How can we expect our ladies to believe if we ourselves are not believing Jesus and His Word? Without Jesus and His Word dwelling in our hearts, we're not going to overflow with Him and His Spirit. Our efforts will certainly ring hollow. Paul puts it this way:

> If I speak in the tongues of men and of angels, but
> have not love, I am a noisy gong or a clanging cymbal.
> *I Corinthians 13:1*

None of us wants to annoy others as a gong gone wrong. But without a personal heart connection to His heart of love, we labor in our own strength. One of my leaders referred to this kind of fruit as being like the "fake grapes" found in her Grandma's kitchen. Rather, we are after the juicy sweet fruit of the Spirit that comes from abiding in the True Vine. To overflow with Christ, one must first abide in Him:

> Abide in me, and I in you. As the branch cannot
> bear fruit by itself, unless it abides in the vine,
> neither can you, unless you abide in me.
> *John 15:4*

Abiding in Jesus is the secret, powerful ingredient to leading Bible study. Okay, maybe it's not so secret, but it is powerful! Some days we feel that heart connection with God and other days we do not, but we can know we are abiding when we are obeying and seeking to follow His will.

Are you daily abiding with The Word from the inside out? Our character and our inner lives ought to align with our outward appearance. There is nothing more effective than a woman leading others with a sanctified and authentic heart. This transformation happens as a woman applies Scripture, yields to God's will and allows for the Spirit's holy work to happen within her own heart. That leads to true beauty. It's attractive. Others will want to follow. Peter says it this way:

> Let your adorning be the hidden person of the heart
> with the imperishable beauty of a gentle and quiet spirit,
> which in God's sight is very precious.
> *I Peter 3:4*

GUARDING YOUR HEART WITH **PRAYER**

Here, again, the need for prayer is likely obvious, but sometimes when we get caught up in the details, we overlook the obvious. Pray, pray, and pray! If Jesus required prayer in order to remain united with the Father in both purpose and mission, surely we need it more. Prayer helps us to stay focused on Christ, the Good Shepherd who leads the way to green pastures. As we study His Word, we desire to follow Christ to these places that teem with His life and living water. However, without Christ to do the heavy lifting of paving the way and clearing the path, we will struggle to get there. And so, we pray.

Set aside time to pray for Bible study. If your schedule allows, before you begin leading this study, take one day away from other activities to commit the weeks ahead to Him.

Remember that prayer is simply sharing your heart and relating with God. It involves both speaking and listening. I find the acronym *P.R.A.Y.* to be useful, especially when praying in groups. This template allows groups to walk through four steps of prayer:

P	PRAISE	Acknowledge your dependence on Him; yield to His ways.

> Blessed are those who have learned to acclaim you,
> who walk in the light of your presence, Lord.
> *Psalm 89:15 NIV*

Beginning a session with praise turns our hearts toward God. In a group setting, I find it effective to encourage short "popcorn prayers" of praise where women take turns utilizing simple words and phrases to worship God. For example:

- I praise You, God, as the Light of the world.
- I praise You for You are mighty to save.
- Lord, You are Life.
- You are the truth.

R	REPENT	Confess and agree with God concerning sin.

> If we confess our sins, he is faithful and just to forgive
> us our sins and to cleanse us from all unrighteousness.
> *I John 1:9*

Offer group members a silent moment to allow for private confession.

A	ADORE	Admire and thank God for His ways.

> Let us come into his presence with thanksgiving;
> let us make a joyful noise to him with songs of praise!
> *Psalm 95:2*

Thanksgiving is a beautiful way to end a Bible study session. Together, give thanks to the Lord for all that He has revealed.

Y	YIELD	Acknowledge your dependence on God. Yield to His ways.

> Whoever abides in me and I in him, he it is that bears much
> fruit, for apart from me you can do nothing. | *John 15:5*
>
> Delight yourself in the Lord, and he will give you the
> desires of your heart. | *Psalm 37:4*

With that, what sorts of things shall we *yield* to God? Here are a few ideas and ways to align with God's heart:

- May God be glorified through the study.
- May God's Will be accomplished in the hearts of women.
- May women know, believe, and abide in Christ.
- May women's hearts be united with His and with one another.
- May God offer protection from all distractions as women commit to studying God's Word.
- May God's Word transform hearts and lives, that women would be holy as He is holy.

GUARDING YOUR HEART WITH **THE WORD**
Read. Reflect. Remember His Word.

Whether teaching a large group or facilitating discussion in a small group, it's easy for leaders to fall into the trap of thinking that we need to have all of the right answers. Furthermore, we often feel the need to be able to speak all those answers eloquently. Due to this false thinking, many leaders spend countless hours scouring commentaries. And we wear ourselves out! After all, God's Word is so deep and rich that we will not plumb the depths of a Scripture passage in just one week. Thinking we need to have all the right answers is a fallacy.

Yes! Without a doubt, commentaries have their valuable place for solid interpretation. (Interpretation is that portion of inductive study where women should all be on the same page.) However, the risk to leaders who spend too much time delving into their commentaries is that the workbook journals plus the teaching and discussion times will reflect the commentaries versus the scripture itself.

To counter this, we simply need time in God's Word. As we read, observe and marinate in the Bible text itself, God's Spirit teaches and leads. His Word speaks on its own. It's powerful and effective. We can trust in it!

> So shall my word be that goes out from my mouth;
> it shall not return to me empty, but it shall
> accomplish that which I purpose, and
> shall succeed in the thing for which I sent it.
> *Isaiah 55:11*

Read, read, and read again. Read the daily Scripture passage using various translations. Read aloud, and read slowly. Ponder. Listen to the Word while driving. Talk about what you are learning and discovering in the Word with family and friends. This will help you be prepared to speak it when time for Bible study. Just as we marinate meat to soften, tenderize, and flavor it, we "sit in" the text allowing God's Spirit to soften, tenderize and flavor our hearts and minds with His personal message.

> I have stored up your word in my heart,
> that I might not sin against you.
> *Psalm 119:11*

A challenging but brilliant way to soak in Scripture is memorization. Memorization is hard work, but the payoff is great. Scripture becomes embedded within us and can overflow from the heart when needed. Certainly, those Scriptures guard my own heart. And in leading, I have noticed that reciting Scripture over women deeply touches their hearts in a way that nothing else does.

Ideally, when studying in groups, teachers and small group leaders should prepare the study a week ahead of time. Yep! You read that right. Seek to be one week ahead of the regular study schedule. Then, allow time for leaders to review together before leading and teaching in groups the following week. The benefits of discussing, sharing, and grappling with the Word as leaders are priceless for preparation and confidence in leading. Also, through that time, God will knit together the hearts of the leaders. That dynamic will then transform the ethos or heart of the group as a whole.

Guarding hearts with Jesus, prayer, and His Word prepares us for life-changing and dynamic conversations around our Bible study tables. In fact, by communing with Jesus and His Spirit through prayer and His Word, you truly have all you need in order to successfully lead a group.

> But you will receive power when the Holy Spirit
> has come upon you, and you will be my witnesses
> in Jerusalem and in all Judea and Samaria,
> and to the end of the earth.
> *Acts 1:8*

The following tools and resources included in this appendix may provide additional help and support as you endeavor to lead your group. Use them however you find them to be helpful.

- Effective Leadership Guide
- Weekly Preparation Guide
- Bible Study Schedule
- Small Group Roster
- Attendance Record
- Prayer Log

effective *leadership*

A GUIDE TO LEADING A SMALL GROUP EFFECTIVELY

Remember that the goal for our study is to see women growing in relationship with Christ and one another. You do not need to be a Bible expert to lead women in discussion about His Word. You only need a heart to love and encourage women. So, what does effective small group leadership look like?

ENCOURAGING | In an *encouraging* small group, all participants feel included and welcome to share freely. Thoughts and ideas are respected, and women are cheered on in their efforts to grow closer to God through their study of His Word.

BIBLICALLY SOUND | When we endeavor to create a *biblically-sound* environment, we point women in the direction of truth and correct doctrine, gently guiding them away from wrong thinking.

BALANCED | In a group that is *balanced*, shy or quiet women are drawn out and encouraged to participate in discussions, while "over-sharers" are encouraged to listen to others and not to dominate the conversation.

WISE | A *wise* small group leader recognizes when the conversation is getting off-topic or veering toward gossip. In such situations, it is a good idea to redirect women back to the ultimate focus of the meeting: God's Word.

PRAYERFUL | A *prayerful* group leader is an asset to her group. She prays regularly for her group members and facilitates opportunities for them to pray for one another.

CONFIDENTIAL | Group members should feel secure that the things they share will remain *confidential*. An effective small group leader is committed to preserving the privacy of her group members.

I AM THE VINE; YOU
ARE THE BRANCHES.
WHOEVER ABIDES IN ME
AND I IN HIM, HE IT IS
THAT BEARS MUCH FRUIT,
FOR APART FROM ME
YOU CAN DO NOTHING.

JOHN 15:5

weekly preparation guide
PREPARING FOR SMALL-GROUP MEETINGS

WEEK ONE | PHILIPPIANS 1

- ☐ Read the assigned daily passages.
- ☐ Use each daily framework to observe, interpret, and apply.
- ☐ Respond to all of the Day 5 questions.
- ☐ Pray for your small group meeting and for your group members.

1 What does this week's study tell me about God?	2 What does this week's study tell me about how I am to relate to Him?

WEEK TWO | PHILIPPIANS 2

- ☐ Read the assigned daily passages.
- ☐ Use each daily framework to observe, interpret, and apply.
- ☐ Respond to all of the Day 5 questions.
- ☐ Pray for your small group meeting and for your group members.

1 What does this week's study tell me about God?	2 What does this week's study tell me about how I am to relate to Him?

WEEK THREE | PHILIPPIANS 3

- ☐ Read the assigned daily passages.
- ☐ Use each daily framework to observe, interpret, and apply.
- ☐ Respond to all of the Day 5 questions.
- ☐ Pray for your small group meeting and for your group members.

1 What does this week's study tell me about God?	2 What does this week's study tell me about how I am to relate to Him?

WEEK FOUR | PHILIPPIANS 4

- ☐ Read the assigned daily passages.
- ☐ Use each daily framework to observe, interpret, and apply.
- ☐ Respond to all of the Day 5 questions.
- ☐ Pray for your small group meeting and for your group members.

1 What does this week's study tell me about God?	2 What does this week's study tell me about how I am to relate to Him?

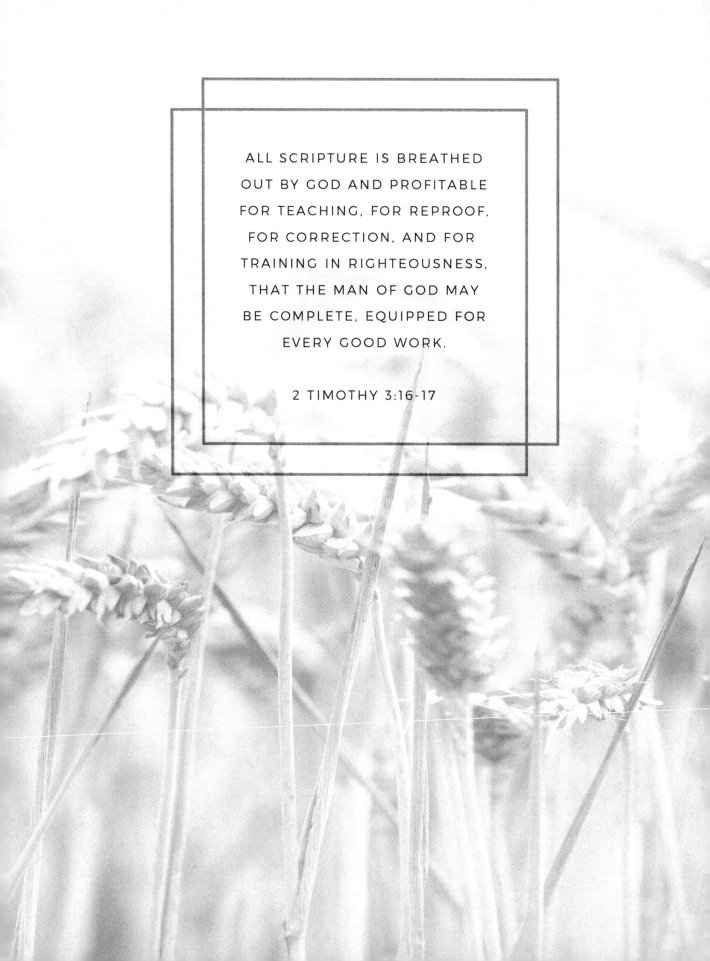

ALL SCRIPTURE IS BREATHED OUT BY GOD AND PROFITABLE FOR TEACHING, FOR REPROOF, FOR CORRECTION, AND FOR TRAINING IN RIGHTEOUSNESS, THAT THE MAN OF GOD MAY BE COMPLETE, EQUIPPED FOR EVERY GOOD WORK.

2 TIMOTHY 3:16-17

bible study *schedule*

PHILIPPIANS | A **SIMPLY BIBLE** STUDY

	READING ASSIGNMENT	SMALL GROUP MEETING DATE	LEADER MEETING DATE
WEEK 1			
WEEK 2			
WEEK 3			
WEEK 4			

small group *roster*

PHILIPPIANS | A **SIMPLY BIBLE** STUDY

PARTICIPANT LIST

1
2
3
4
5
6
7
8
9
10
11
12
13

NAME	
BIRTHDAY PHONE NUMBER EMAIL ADDRESS CONTACT METHOD	
NOTES	

NAME	
BIRTHDAY PHONE NUMBER EMAIL ADDRESS CONTACT METHOD	
NOTES	

NAME	
BIRTHDAY PHONE NUMBER EMAIL ADDRESS CONTACT METHOD	
NOTES	

NAME	
BIRTHDAY PHONE NUMBER EMAIL ADDRESS CONTACT METHOD	
NOTES	

NAME	
BIRTHDAY PHONE NUMBER EMAIL ADDRESS CONTACT METHOD	
NOTES	

NAME	
BIRTHDAY PHONE NUMBER EMAIL ADDRESS CONTACT METHOD	
NOTES	

NAME	
BIRTHDAY PHONE NUMBER EMAIL ADDRESS CONTACT METHOD	
NOTES	

NAME

BIRTHDAY
PHONE NUMBER
EMAIL ADDRESS
CONTACT METHOD

NOTES

NAME

BIRTHDAY
PHONE NUMBER
EMAIL ADDRESS
CONTACT METHOD

NOTES

NAME

BIRTHDAY
PHONE NUMBER
EMAIL ADDRESS
CONTACT METHOD

NOTES

attendance *log*

PHILIPPIANS | A **SIMPLY BIBLE** STUDY

PARTICIPANT'S NAME	WEEK 1 | PHILIPPIANS 1	WEEK 2 | PHILIPPIANS 2	WEEK 3 | PHILIPPIANS 3	WEEK 4 | PHILIPPIANS 4
1				
2				
3				
4				
5				
6				
7				
8				
9				
10				
11				
12				
13				

prayer *log*

PHILIPPIANS | A **SIMPLY BIBLE** STUDY

DATE	NAME	REQUEST	FOLLOW-UP

DATE	NAME	REQUEST	FOLLOW-UP

DATE	NAME	REQUEST	FOLLOW-UP

DATE	NAME	REQUEST	FOLLOW-UP

DATE	NAME	REQUEST	FOLLOW-UP

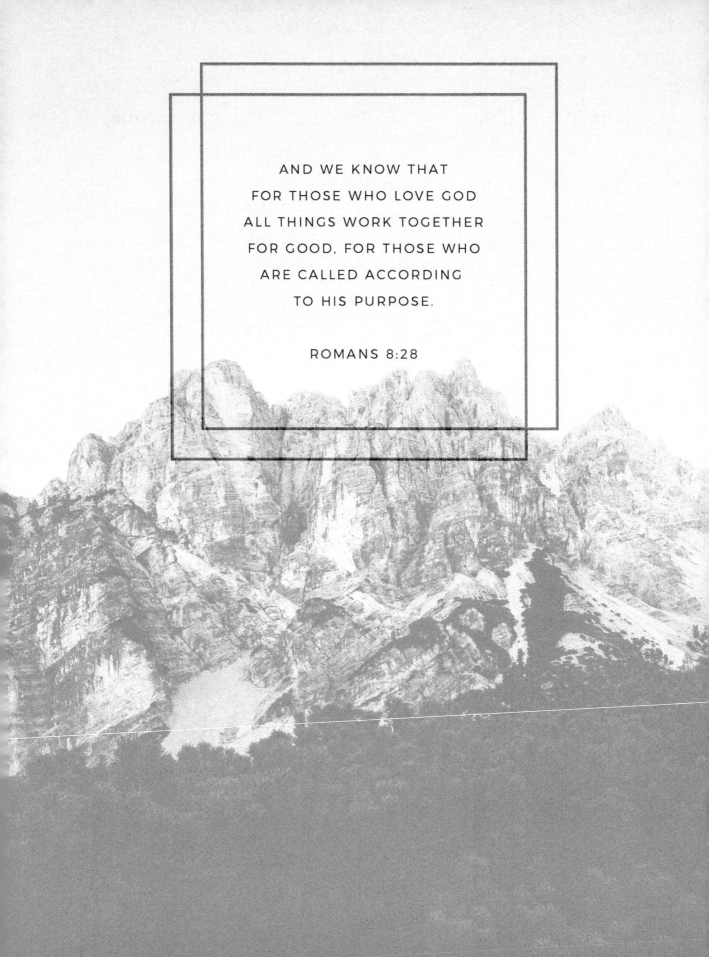

Made in the USA
Middletown, DE
21 February 2019